Collections of Salem

Salem Eckert

BookLeaf Publishing

Presentation by *BookLeaf Publishing*

Web: www.bookleafpub.com

E-mail: info@bookleafpub.com

ISBN: 9789357613675

First edition 2022

To everyone struggling to balance their plates, those who need help and feel like they can't get it. It will come, I know it will.

ACKNOWLEDGEMENT

I would like to thank all who I love, and all who love me. There are many special people in my life and without them I wouldn't be here today. Thank you for giving me life.

PREFACE

As a single non-binary person I struggle to find comfort, love and belonging. This book will take you through 21 days of my life juggling work, dating, mental health and friendships.

Change

a
signal of change
comes about
airing only revision
of past errors
made on a
quite consistent basis.
Revised
just to make
n e w   e r r o r s .

Albeit
cyclical,
constantly renewing.

Airing
revising
error.

Question

Faded, muted, unborn
Not hurt, but broken
overpowered by
an utter distaste for a vessel
carrying gratuitously
the aggregate of
you.

Questions
unanswered neglected,
disregarded queries
accruing rapidly

daily,
hourly,
instantaneously,
continuously,

harassing the nature of
you.

Finally amounting
to the insurmountable.

Months,
years
pass by vehemently

until

the posing of a

s i n g l e q u e s t i o n

extinguishes all
doubt.

An understanding is
apprehended.

Memories of...

I will miss him
more than I have missed
anyone before.

When the time comes I will be...

lost.

Lost, in a city I have lived in my whole life.
Lost, in a home I've made to be my own.
Lost, in a body I have grown in for 24 years.

I hope that I will find peace.
I hope that I can move on,
living my life
like I had never met him.

But I know,
that life would be so empty
and loveless.

Hoping for Progress

Expeditiously, a smile crossed thine face,
remembering freeness I had before,
now wishing it were once again the case,
but why don't I feel this way anymore?

Pondering this thought I deeply wonder.
How can I feel so closed and afraid?
Now I ask when did my life asunder,
and when were these changes suddenly made?

A realization has now occurred,
to recognize the power I carry.
Now feeling appreciably affirmed,
an end to the the shame I needed to bury.

I am choosing to love my existence,
working for progress no matter distance.

Cheap Vacation

Clearing my evening schedule to
have just a few
ending up having a few more than a few,
always wondering if my idea of
pampering fits the definition.

Vivaciously living
although some may say, drunk
continuing my pattern,
accruing more and more
thinking...
is this too much?
only time will tell
now fully enjoying my cheap vacation.

Rain

Water falling

collecting freely on land

refreshing all life

Distant

The sweet memories whisk by,
like the wind in your hair.

You can see it all,
feel it all.
everything you've ever loved.

Jubilation.

then a sudden fading,
as if those memories were decades ago,
too far to feel real.

Are you broken?
What could have caused this?
This wrench from exultation?

Loneliness encroaches again,
has the depression set back in?

October 6 2022

I hope he'll remember I love him still
when the time comes
through my tears, I think he will

the early morn chill,
desperate for the way it numbs,
I hope he will remember I love him still.

every word I speak is so shrill,
sensing the air expelling from my lungs,
Through my tears, I think he will.

feeling profoundly ill;
too much it all becomes,
I hope he'll remember I love him still,
through my tears, I think he will

For a Lifetime

10

Such intensity
I have never felt before
So deep and divine
Holding on for a lifetime
Knowing to be greatly missed

A Place

I have come,
I have come to a place.

A place where I feel safe.
A place that I can cry.

I have come,
I have come to a place.

A place where I can embrace, me.
A place that I can feel, deeper.

I have never felt this before.

It feels so beautiful,
but also,
so, so heavy.

I have come,
I have come to a place.

Soulmates

I believe,
we have more than one soulmate.

More than one person,
who makes life worth living,
simply by existing.

More than one person,
who warms your soul,
from any distance.

More than one person,
who makes breathing air,
so much easier.

However...

I can't imagine anyone else but you.

more than one person,
and I choose you.
Every. Damn. Time.

Grown

Every morning grows colder and colder.

Hoping this year will be better than the last,
so much heartbreak,
death and struggle.

Worry sets in.
Have I grown since then?

I still make mistakes...
Have I really learned?

I would argue...
Argue?
With who?

I have grown.
I have got through these struggles,
but I have seen the sun.
I have touched the grass.
I have felt the wind on my face.

I have grown,
Into a strong person,
who can,

and will,
carry on.

Survival

I have survived,
for many years.

24 to be exact.

Everyday keeping my nose just above the water,
struggling to breathe,
eyes closed,
just fighting,
to stay above the water.

Some days wishing I would just,
sink.

Some days,
trying to sink.

But,
I tread,
continuously,
everyday,
to exhaustion.

Dreaming of the day I can stand,
on my own two feet.

Feeling the sand between my toes,
sun on my skin,
warmth.

All the while,
whilst I was dreaming,
whilst I was hoping,
I was floating and treading to shore.

I haven't made it to shore,
but,
I can see it now.

I have been in survival for so long,
and now...

my feet can almost touch the bottom,
I just need to keep treading a little longer,
but its becoming easier,
I feel so much lighter.

The water feels warmer,
almost friendly...

I think...

I'll make it.

Rejection

Theres nothing worse,
than putting yourself out there,
for no one to enjoy you for who you are.

Nothing worse than someone,
not wanting to be in your life,
when their existence,
makes your life worth living.

Theres nothing worse than being so close,
but unable to reach.

I feels like there is nothing worse,
than being,
unloved.

The Greatest Feeling

I have never felt so free.

I have never felt so joyous.

I have never felt so elated,
as I did on that rollercoaster.

To feel the wind in my face,
my hands gripping the bar,
tighter than I've ever held anything before.

The freedom I felt was so immense.

I wish was filled with that feeling,
filled with freedom,
filled with elation,
filled with joy.

I think it would make the hard days,
just a little easier,
knowing I would have,
another rollercoaster moment.

Instead, I crave it.

struggling to find the happiness and excitement
in everyday life.

I just wish,
I could feel that freedom every time I really
needed it.

Than They Used To

Sometimes I forget,
I am in a way better place,
than I was before.

Even though every day seems hard,
these days are so much,
easier than they used to be.

Fucking Men

I cannot make a statement of all men,
as I have not met every man.

However,
Why does every man,
I have ever,
truly loved,
left.

To far away lands I may never visit.
To new places I cannot afford to live in.

Why must they do this to me?
Why must they be so,
perfectly unavailable.

A Drunken Night

I come to you drunk.

Tonight.

Sweaty,
stinky,
partied out.

But honest.

I am so tired.

Tired of playing this game.
This game of love.

I think this is my last time,
that I put myself on the line.

For nothing but the comfort of another.
I don't know if I can do it,
again.

But here I am,
drunk.
trying again,

again,
and again.

Wasting so many minutes,
falling in love with someone,
who will run away again.

Leaving me emptier than before,
but helping me learn,
my own company...

just may be best.

Living Well

I have made a decision,

to meet my own needs.

Making plans to do only good things for myself.
Taking care of,
me.

Tomorrow I will wake with peace in my heart,
determination in my soul,
and motivation in my mind.

I promise to live well.

BrickHouse

25

Brickhouse mindset now

learn how to love this body

Working towards growth

Ode To Us

We have made it so far!

We have made it to October 1st, 2022.

This is an Ode To Us.

So many years,
we have suffered.

Now were thriving,
living to the fullest.

Doing things that make our heart beat.
Doing things to make us healthy humans.
Doing things to make us...
happy.

Making changes that benefit...
us.

Doing nothing but making us,
the best people we can be.

Isn't it amazing?

How we do the things that make us so happy?
How we did the things we've always wanted?
How we make good choices for ourselves?

I'm so proud of us and how far we've come.

You're growing everyday, and I have never been
more proud...

of us.